Day-To-Day Happiness

A simple and effective guide to happier thinking, happier language and a happier you.

About the Author

Beau Bridgland is a young, English voice actor for animation, video games, commercials, narration and more. Despite having a very happy childhood, during his time at university he developed a deep depression, severe anxiety and low self-esteem. Following this, Beau has been on a relentless pursuit of happiness in a quest to learn all he can about it. As a result he has been able to actively chase his dreams, has gone on many wonderful adventures and has never been happier.

Beau Bridgland

Day- To- Day Happiness

Olympia Publishers
London

www.olympiapublishers.com
OLYMPIA PAPERBACK EDITION

A CIP catalogue record for this title is
available from the British Library.

ISBN: 978-1-84897-826-3

This is a work of fiction.
Names, characters, places and incidents originate from the writer's
imagination. Any resemblance to actual persons, living or dead, is
purely coincidental.

First Published in 2017

Olympia Publishers
60 Cannon Street
London
EC4N 6NP

Printed in Great Britain

CONTENTS

FOREWORD

It is quite a remarkable thing to meet someone and instantly feel as though you have known them forever. It is also a blessing, which was the case when I first met Beau. I was immediately struck by his courage and determination, but soon grew to admire the kind and gentle man inside. When we talked for hours and he shared with me his dreams, his heart's desires and his difficult struggles, I knew that our meeting was meant to be. It was obvious from that first meeting that his heart and compassion for others is very large. With this wonderful book, he is sharing from his soul the challenges he has faced in order to help those who may be walking along the same road. And, he is doing it for the right reason... he really wants to make a difference in those lives. After you have read his loving, caring and wise words, I know you will have a similar opinion of my amazing young friend as I do. And, I know he will change your life for the better – just like he changed mine.

Penny Abshire

Founder of Positive Thinkers UNITE

www.positivethinkersunite.com

WHO AM I?

My name is Beau Bridgland; I am a young, English voice actor for animation, video games, commercials, narration and more. My dream is to go to Los Angeles to further my voice acting career. In the past few years I have travelled to America several times, been to awesome places such as Nickelodeon Animation Studio and met and learned from many of my heroes in the business. Right now, I am very close to moving to the USA and I am very happy. But when it really comes down to it...

I'm just an ordinary guy. I went to a normal school and had a regular upbringing. Though I was a bit shy at times, I had lots of friends and hobbies. Overall, I had a very happy childhood. Yet during my time at university I became incredibly unhappy and felt worse than I had ever felt before. I developed a deep depression, severe anxiety and seriously low self-esteem, all of which plagued me every day for over two years.

When university ended and I still felt as bad as ever, I realised this was different to anything I had experienced before. It wasn't going to go away by itself and I had to do something. Ever since, I have relentlessly pursued happiness in a quest to discover what was making me feel this way, why I hadn't felt like this before, what I could do to stop it and what I could do to try and prevent it coming back.

WHAT IS THIS? WHO IS THIS FOR?

This book contains what I learned during my quest for happiness. It is a collection of what has helped me get to where I am today; what has helped others; what to avoid and what to strive for. All put in a short, simplistic way.

This book is for anyone who wants help dealing with the off-moments and difficult days in life. It is my hope that this helps anyone who feels: sad, down, anxious, fed up, dread, useless, hopeless, guilty, scared, apathetic, unfulfilled or that something in their life is just a bit out of place. Whether you are a bit depressed or have full on depression, I hope this can help you in some way.

Particularly for those with very serious and intense problems, this book is intended as a supplement – and not a substitution – for going to a doctor and having cognitive behavioural therapy. Also, if you are having _any_ thoughts on suicide at all, **_go see a doctor immediately_**.

This book is not about preventing all bad things from happening. It's not about never feeling crummy again. You're never going to always feel happy, just as you are never going to always feel sad or angry.

A shield can never truly defend you from absolutely everything. A shield is not damage proof but is, more accurately, damage resistant. They will defend you against some attacks and lessen the impact of others. A good shield provides confidence; it lets you enter a world of potentially difficult, intimidating and off-putting situations and lets you know that you will come out of it okay.

This book aims to provide just that: a shield.

WRITING THINGS DOWN

Frequently throughout this book, I will suggest making a list or writing things down. Please, please, please, do *physically write things down*. Buy a special notebook if you need to.

For a start, writing things down allows you to slow down your thinking enough for you to actually acknowledge it. The awareness of your thoughts will increase.

You gain a new perspective on your thoughts, feelings and beliefs once they are out there, written down. Looking over them (or even reading them aloud) makes them feel very different from how they seemed inside your mind. Many types of irrational or warped thinking are discussed in this book; if you recognise any of them in your own thinking, write them down next to your thoughts.

Finally, when you have things written down, you can see the progress you make and potentially chart it.

EASIER SAID THAN DONE

As you read this, you may often think, "Well that's easier said than done" and often, you'll probably be right.

A lot of these suggestions are things that you do automatically when you are happy. Yet when you are unhappy, their opposites become your habits. It can become incredibly difficult to stay focused on the good things. Your mind starts thinking in an illogical and unreasonable way, clouding your judgment.

So I understand how change can be tough but please just try this stuff out. Find the bits you like and agree with, and stick with them. Soon enough, you will notice a positive difference.

HOW WE THINK IS HOW WE FEEL

Our emotions are the direct result of our thoughts. It is not what happens to us that affects how we feel but actually how we think about it. If we change how we think about something, we change our emotional reaction. You may not believe me, so consider this:

Imagine your phone starts ringing and you don't recognize the number.

You may feel angry – you are confident it will be someone trying to sell you something.

You may feel nervous – it could be that company you just had a job interview with.

You may get excited – that girl you really liked and gave your number to three nights ago might be trying to call you.

You may become scared – your dad did say your mum had been coughing more lately, what if it's to do with that?

You may just be mildly curious – "I wonder what this could be? I'm intrigued as to how they got my number."

These are all realistic responses. Bear this in mind though: in every case, all you are reacting to is a little machine making a noise, the rest you have invented. You thought about what it could be and those thoughts led to anger, nervousness, excitement and so on.

AUTOMATIC THOUGHTS

We all have automatic thoughts, the little words and pictures that jump into our heads, the little quick decisions and judgments we make. They are the ones largely responsible for our feelings. Some automatic thoughts are good; others are bad. Some examples of bad ones include:

"I'm stupid."

"I could never do anything that cool."

"What if he doesn't find it funny?"

The first thing you need to do is become aware of your automatic thoughts. Write them down. Knowing what your thoughts are will help you change them.

You can't just choose what all of your automatic thoughts will be at a moment's notice. However, if you follow the advice outlined in this book, with practice and time you can ultimately change how those automatic thoughts will generally behave, which will improve how you feel.

BE KIND TO YOURSELF

Treat yourself the way you would want others to treat you. Remember, not only does everyone make mistakes but that lots of people out there make the same mistakes you do. Go easy on yourself, give yourself a break, you're only human.

You might think to yourself or say something like, "I'm so stupid" or "I'm never going to get this, I'm useless!" Imagine if you followed a friend around all day saying things like that to them. You wouldn't, would you? It's neither kind nor motivating.

Ask yourself these questions when you have automatic thoughts:

Would I say that to a friend?

Is it helpful to think/say that?

Does it make me happy to think/say that?

BAD THINGS HAPPEN

Don't get me wrong, I am not saying that there is no such thing as a bad event. Bad things exist and bad things happen. For there to be an up, there must also exist a down; for there to be a better, there must exist a worse, it's a law of the universe.

Sometimes, lots of genuinely bad things will be thrown at you all in one go and you won't be able to help it, it's out of your control.

However, some things are not as bad as they seem, some may not really be bad at all and lots of bad things with enough time can even become good.

So when bad things happen, it's okay to feel sad or bad. There is nothing wrong with that, you're only human. In fact, even after you have reasonably analysed a situation and intellectually understood that everything is all right, it can still take time for your heart to catch up to your head, to take it all in and feel okay again.

WARNING SIGNS

Often, emotional changes in your life can be accompanied by physical ones. If life is getting you down, you could notice aches, pains or changes in:

Tiredness

Quality of sleep

Amount of sleep

Sex drive

Appetite

Weight

Try to be aware of these changes and make a note of any personal patterns. If you then notice any of these physical changes, it can alert you to something not quite being right in your life emotionally. At my most depressed, I was underweight and thirteen percent lighter than I am now.

UPS, DOWNS AND IMPROVEMENT

Imagine a student who before her exam does one practice paper each day for ten days. This chart shows her scores:

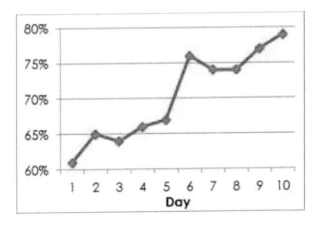

I think almost everyone would say that (overall) she improved. Yet if you look at this chart, there were some times where her score dropped or stayed the same.

Nobody literally improves each and every time they do something. We all slip back a bit sometimes. We all have a little run of bad form from time-to-time before bouncing back.

If on one individual occasion or for a little while you regress, that is completely fine; it's not the end of the world. So whether you're trying to lose weight, score higher on a test or improve your life some other way, look at the bigger picture and remember your progress on the whole.

BLACK AND WHITE THINKING

Be aware of when you speak or think in a "black and white" way with an "all-or-nothing" attitude. Examples include:

"I *always* mess up *everything*."

"I *never* have *any* luck in *anything*."

"I am a *total* idiot."

"*Everyone* will hate me."

Think about it though: you don't *always* mess up at *everything* you do. If you rated how well you did *everything* you do on a scale of 0 to 10, would you give *everything* a 0? There are some things that at the very least you are okay at doing. We all have *some* luck; nobody is stupid in *every* conceivable way and there are over seven billion people in the world, would *every one of them* really go as far as hating you?

When you really give it some thought, there really isn't much in the universe that is totally one way or totally the other, there is middle ground in-between. Would you call a person who fails their school exams but is able to fix all your computer problems totally stupid? Probably not. So watch out when you use words like these:

Always	Never	Completely
Nothing	All	Worst
Totally	Every	Impossible

Instead, avoid exaggeration, look at the grey in-between area and remember that there are lots of different ways you can be or not be something.

RED. AMBER. GREEN

Remember that there is a difference between "like", "didn't like" and "dislike" or between, "good", "not good", "not bad" and "bad". If someone says they "didn't like" something, don't assume it means they hated it. Pay close attention to these kinds of differences.

I often like to think of a traffic light system. *Green* things are good, you like and enjoy them. *Amber* things are okay, you wouldn't say you enjoy them but you wouldn't say you dislike them either. *Red* things are bad; you dislike them and find them unenjoyable.

Fill your life with as much green as possible. Fill the rest with amber and avoid red things. Try to remove the red from your life as best you can.

MEASUREMENTS AND SPECIFICITY

Using measurements and being specific is a good way of avoiding exaggeration, remembering the grey in-between and remaining level-headed.

If there is anything that you can put a number to, scale or chart, do it. It really helps when you have some kind of result that you can measure and evaluate.

If you think, "I don't have *any* good friends" then make a list of all the *specific* things a "good friend" is and then see if anyone you know meets those criteria. You will most likely find that at least one person will. If not, are your expectations of a "good friend" realistic? Would those people be a "good friend" to anybody else according to your standards? Are you a "good friend" to anyone according to that list?

Imagine a man who wants to be healthier, so he tries to lose weight. For the first three weeks he does but during week four he puts on two pounds and says, "I am the *worst* dieter *ever*!"

Yes, according to the specific measurement, he has not achieved his goal and in fact done the opposite. But is he *truly* the *worst* dieter *ever*? Has *nobody* else *ever* gained weight on a diet? In fact, there is probably someone else out there who has gained more than two pounds in a week whilst they are on a diet.

Plus, there are other factors the man could measure to assess his health. He could additionally measure and chart his waist length and the amount of exercise he can do.

Also ensure that any measurements you take are relative to you. Someone much heavier than the man from before will find it easier to lose two pounds than he will.

Really examine what you say and think to see if it really is true or not.

DON'T FIXATE ON THE NEGATIVE

In everything that happens, there are good and bad elements. Particularly when you are depressed, you can form a very poor habit of singling out the negative parts and focusing on them exclusively.

A student may feel sad about their fantastic exam results due to one bad grade. A tasty meal can be ignored because of one overcooked component. A sportsperson can feel an entire game went badly after one small mistake they made at the very end.

An upcoming meeting with your boss can lead to you believing you will be fired – even though you don't know what the meeting will be about. One possible negative outcome has been chosen and tenaciously fixated on.

I'M NOT BEING NEGATIVE, I'M BEING REALISTIC

Lots of people say, "I'm not being negative, I'm being realistic". In fact I used to, until I realised that ninety-nine percent of the time, when I or someone else said this, we *were* being negative, we *weren't* being realistic.

I even noticed that this phrase is often used after someone says a sentence with "never" or "always" or something similar in it.

If after hearing that you still think you are the one percent then it is likely you are still being negative.

Fixating on one, undesirable outcome and saying it *will* happen, nothing else – is being negative. Being aware of all the potential outcomes of a situation and understanding that *any* of them can happen – is being realistic. Being realistic whilst remaining hopeful that the *good* potential outcomes will happen – is being positive.

DON'T PLAY DOWN THE POSITIVE

Don't ignore the positives and don't disqualify, downplay or devalue them either. When looking at a positive in a situation or when someone congratulates you, try to avoid saying anything such as:

That doesn't count	Anybody could do it	It's not a big deal
It was nothing	Yeah but that's easy	They're just being nice
It doesn't matter	Oh I was just lucky	It is not important

Understand that not everybody can do everything, appreciate the skill it takes to achieve something and be thankful for the good stuff.

FINDING THE POSITIVES

When something bad happens and it greatly affects you, make a physical list of all the positives of that situation – in particular, the lessons you can learn from that experience. It is harder to do this for some events than it is for others. For some things, it may take time for you to understand and experience the positives.

For past events, think back to what you learned from those experiences – such as what to avoid doing if anything like that happens to you again or to a friend. Also think of what good things couldn't have happened without them – not a lot of people marry their first romantic partner, they have to go through a number of relationships first before finding the person they want to spend the rest of their life with. Try to find three positives for each bad past experience. If you can't find three, then that might just mean not enough time has passed yet.

For events in the present or future, think of similar past situations, how you got through them before and how you can again. Think of friends who have gotten through it. Know that anything worth doing comes with its challenges.

Another useful skill is being able to find the win-win...

FINDING THE WIN-WIN

Regardless of what happens in life, you want to always be able to find something good to cling onto.

If a student does well on a practice exam, that's great and means they are well-prepared. If they make mistakes, then they are alerted to what areas they need to focus on or what to watch out for on the real test.

When you are uncertain about the future and what lies next, make a list of all the possible outcomes you can imagine and find a positive within each one. Then whatever does happen will be a win in some way.

WHAT'S THE WORST THAT COULD HAPPEN?

If you are feeling anxious about the future, ask yourself: what do you feel is the worst that could happen? Write it down. If there are other outcomes you come up with, write those down too. There are two things you can then do:

Evaluate the realism and likelihood.

Plan for it.

How likely is it for that to happen? Has it happened to you before? Has it happened to many others before? Is it actually realistic? You might realise you are worrying about something ridiculous. Carefully analyse what you are thinking about and if it is logical. However, if you still feel concerned, make a plan. At the very least, plan the first thing you will do if that outcome happens.

A student may worry about not getting the exam results they want and panic that it could result in them getting a job they don't like.

However, the student may not need many points to get what they want. They have a good track record in that subject and have been doing well in mock tests. Their worries could be relatively unjustified.

The student can then make a plan, just in case. In the event that the student does not get the result they want, there is still a lot that they can do. If their grade is quite close to what they wanted, they can get the paper remarked. Alternatively, they could prepare to sit the exam again next summer and delay any future plans for a little while, such as attending university.

If the student is still worried about a bad job, they have to go back to questioning the realism and likelihood. Not everyone who is successful gets good results in school, just as not every person who gets good grades in school is guaranteed a successful future. If they get a job they don't like, they can always work hard in their free time to find another one or earn a qualification.

DON'T FOCUS ON THE FUTURE

Life is incredibly unpredictable, isn't it? Plans are cancelled, dates are changed, what we think will happen so often turns out to be wrong. So it very naturally follows: don't make predictions.

The future is constantly changing. You have a safe job, then you are suddenly made redundant but then a friend knows a guy looking to hire someone exactly like you.

We often feel a crushing disappointment due to something not being what we expected. We feel bad only because of an incorrect assumption we made. Additionally, lots of things we worry about happening never even occur.

Yes, be aware of what could happen so that you can prepare but don't start assuming any of it will happen. Try to live life with a "let's just see how this goes" attitude.

DON'T FOCUS ON THE PAST

Once something has happened, you can't change it – it's over, it's done, it can't hurt you, it's in the past.

Just because something happened once, does not mean it will happen again, sometimes things happen randomly or as a one-off coincidence. You can learn lessons, reflect on mistakes and this alone can change the future.

For each thing you have done in the past, remember this: you did it because at that time you thought it was the best decision. It's not your fault if in time a decision turns out not to be the best one.

Finally, don't hold onto what you used to have or to some life that may have been.

FOCUS ON THE PRESENT

Sometimes we can be sitting around, watching TV but feeling concerned about something that happened or worrying about something that might yet happen. A really good question to ask is:

In this moment, right now, am I safe? When you really think about it, usually in any given moment, we are actually okay.

We are in our homes, in a comfortable or secure environment, with people we love, doing something we find fun or are used to doing. What happened before isn't happening anymore and what could happen in the future isn't happening now, and may never happen either.

IS IT IMPORTANT?

When you find yourself stuck with a thought, which you keep going over and over in your mind, evaluate its importance.

You spill your drink during a meal out and you find it quite embarrassing. Ask: will this still matter next week? What about in a month? What about in a year? Two years? Three years? Five years? Ten years?

Try to question if the thing you are worrying about really matters. Is it life and death? Or is it just a very small detail that won't really affect anything much? You are writing a shopping list and make a mistake, which annoys you. Yes, you have an ugly looking cross on your list but can you still read it? Were you going to keep that list forever?

THINK ABOUT SOMETHING ELSE

Once you rationalise a thought, it can still take a while for you to stop thinking about it.

If I said, "Don't think about green monkeys", the first thing you think of is green monkeys. They may even now be stuck in your head. For the same reason, it's best to resist the temptation of saying to yourself, "Don't think about that".

A more effective technique is to actually think of something else, something good. You can choose to think of the positive side of something, such as all the ways that job interview went right or how awesome it would be to get that job. Alternatively, just focus on something else entirely, such as something you are looking forward to, a song you love or your breathing – inhaling for a few seconds, holding for a few seconds and then exhaling for a few seconds. Or you can think about green monkeys.

JUDGE YOUR ACTIONS, NOT YOURSELF

You accidentally drop a glass and it smashes. You think, "*I'm an idiot!*" Almost everyone has accidentally broken something at some point. Doing so doesn't make you an idiot. What you really mean is, "*That* was idiotic!"

Don't judge your entire self because of one action or event. Instead, judge the actions themselves. At times it can be as simple as replacing the "I am" with "that was".

Remember as well, there are lots of different ways a person can be clever, nice, successful, attractive (inside and out), talented and so on. Be careful with your labels and avoid labelling a person *completely*.

UNFAIRNESS AND ANGER

Anger for the most part, stems from a sense of unfairness. Unfairness in that we feel something shouldn't happen. Like it or not, life is not always going to be fair.

It feels unfair that people live in poverty or get laid off despite being good workers. People may feel hard done by when they behave well and follow the rules whilst others get away with breaking them.

Like other emotions, it is okay to feel anger; it is not necessarily a bad emotion. However, there is a time and a place for it. There are two helpful questions to ask:

Is it useful?

Is it justified?

Will your anger help your goal? A typically quiet person's anger during an argument may let the other person know that they are very serious about what they are talking about, which is helpful. On the other hand, getting angry in a traffic jam never makes you go any faster.

Is it actually unfair? Getting angry that you didn't get hired for a job is not really justified, as lots of people apply for the same jobs and only one person can get each. They are not saying you wouldn't be good for the job but are just choosing someone else who they felt was better suited for it, it's selection not rejection and thus not really unfair. An athlete losing to another that cheated however is against the rules and is unfair.

There is another question you may want to consider asking as well:

HAVE I DONE EVERYTHING IN MY POWER?

You can release a huge amount of anger or anxious tension by asking yourself: have I done everything in my power?

Is there more you could do? Try to make a list of what else you realistically could do to improve the situation. If you don't come up with anything and feel there's nothing more you can do, accept that. Once you have done your best and all you can do, know that the rest is out of your control, so it's not worth worrying about. What will be, will be.

If what you come up with is quick and easy to do, do it now. If it's a bit more complicated, make a plan to do it or at least plan the next step to doing it. Simply knowing the immediate next step brings a huge amount of relief.

VALUE YOURSELF

Put yourself first. Your time and your energy are precious. It is not selfish to do something for yourself. Selfishness is doing *everything* for yourself with *no* regard for others.

People have respect for those who have respect for themselves. Nothing you do is a waste of time. You are never wasting anyone else's time. People wouldn't talk to you, write messages to you or invest their precious time and energy into you if they didn't want to or if they disliked you. Even people you pay to help you in some way could just walk away or refuse service.

You are not useless, worthless or hopeless (these are black and white terms). Nobody has the exact same genetics and experiences as you and nobody ever will. You are incredibly unique!

YOU ARE VALUABLE TO OTHERS

We all have strengths and weaknesses, not everyone is good at everything. Therefore there are things you can do that others can't and so you have things to offer others.

Even if you feel that many others share the same skills as you, consider that those others have different combinations of skills and levels of ability. They still can't do what you do in quite the same way.

There are talents you have to work for and some that come more naturally but they all count. Know your strengths and weaknesses. Keep those strengths strong and work on improving the weaknesses.

SAYING SORRY

When we don't like the idea of disappointing others we can be very quick to say sorry, sometimes before we have even done anything wrong. If you find yourself saying sorry or about to say sorry, answer first: what have I done wrong?

If it is for something that hasn't even happened yet, don't say sorry. Don't assume you are going to do something wrong or are going to be a disappointment. If it's for something you nearly did wrong, then you didn't do anything wrong.

Has someone confronted you about the problem expressing disappointment or anger towards you? Or do you just think they might be annoyed?

Are you even involved at all? Don't take responsibility for anything you are not actually involved with.

LEARN WHEN TO SAY NO

Part of respecting yourself is learning when to say no.

If you really do not want to do something or feel it would be wrong, say no and explain. Friends usually understand and will be okay with it. They aren't demanding you to do something.

Sometimes people just ask you to do something because they had already asked your friends and didn't want you to feel left out. They don't mind whether you do or don't but were just checking.

If someone asks again, tell them no again and if they keep pushing, keep saying no. Don't be afraid to tell them that you have already told them no and that they are starting to be rude if they continue to persist. They may not even realise.

LEARN WHEN TO SAY YES

Sometimes we don't feel worthy enough to say yes. If you want something *and* it is offered to you, there is nothing wrong with accepting it, say yes.

If you want to say yes to an offer but feel it is also incredibly generous, it is fine to ask once, "Is that okay?" or "Are you sure?" or state "Because I really don't mind..." but if they still say yes, don't ask again or refuse, accept it.

When you do something nice for someone else, it gives you a sense of joy and accomplishment. Refusing to accept a gift robs a person of that, so only refuse an offer when it is something you don't want. If someone is insistent on doing something you don't want to do, compromise and find an alternative.

ACCEPTING PRAISE AND DESERVING SUCCESS

Valuing yourself and learning to say yes are the foundations of learning to accept praise and feel deserving of success.

If someone thanks you or gives you a compliment and you reject it, you are robbing them of a moment of happiness. Instead, simply say, "Thank you" or "You're welcome" or "Happy to help".

Just because something is simple for you, does not mean it is simple for someone else. Something insignificant to you could mean the world to someone else. You have something that they don't have and that they needed. You may have worked really hard for a long time to develop a particular skill, so don't feel bad about it.

Their gratitude is genuine, this means their praise and your success are as well. What they think about you is true for them, so don't argue against it and don't feel concerned about the idea of a person somehow potentially over-evaluating you. Unless you did something unethical to get it, don't feel guilty about your success, enjoy it.

DON'T FORGET THE GOOD

It can be easy to forget the good things when something bad comes along. When we feel happy, it's easier to recall happy memories; when we're sad, it's easier to remember sad ones and so on. If a talented sportsperson plays badly one game, they may remember other mistakes and think, "I'm a terrible player!"

In times such as these, make a list of all the things that show this is wrong. List all of the times you played well, the times people praised you, any awards you may have received, any time anyone went the extra mile for you because you aren't a terrible player.

Don't throw everything good out of the window at the sight of one bad thing. Always hold onto the good and never forget it.

LOOK AT WHAT YOU HAVE DONE, NOT WHAT YOU HAVE YET TO DO

When you have a goal, regardless of how big or small, always think of how far you have come and not how far you have left to go.

You can easily get overwhelmed when you think about all of the things you hope to do but haven't. You can start criticising yourself and blaming yourself for not having done them yet.

Focus instead on what you have done so far, recall the challenges involved and how you overcame them, think of just how much you have really accomplished, particularly since some journeys are ongoing.

"POTENTIAL"

The idea of potential is so often mentioned in a negative way, "I haven't lived up to my potential" or "You had the potential to be a doctor" for instance.

Consider the "potential" to be a doctor. How would a person be sure that you could have passed all of the necessary exams? Get all the required qualifications? Keep up with the ever changing world of medicine? Have that personal touch? Cope with long hours? Most importantly, do they know if doing all of that – going on the journey to become a doctor – would make you happy?

How could they know all that? What is that specifically based on? What are they measuring? What does potential even mean?

The other side of having "potential" is living up to it. However, we've pointed out "potential" is quite a weak concept. How can you live up to something that barely exists? Even if it did, what if there is potential you don't even know you have? At what point can you say you have fulfilled your potential? Finally, just because we *could* do something, doesn't mean we *should*.

Concentrate on the qualities, skills or attributes you possess that could make you good at something rather than the idea of potential. If someone else starts talking about your potential, ask them what they really mean.

Focus on what you want to do instead of what you think you possibly, maybe, sort of, potentially could be.

MIND READING

Can you read other peoples' minds? Can you literally hear their thoughts? No? Then don't assume what other people are thinking.

Often we imagine or invent what another person is thinking. We imagine that a person has demanded we do something that they have never actually demanded. Or we assume what they will say to us the next time we speak to them.

Picture this: a girl may think that her mother wants her to go into the family business. She thinks her mum expects her to go to college. She feels that when she tells her mum she's not going to college and instead wants to be an artist, her mum will be unhappy and lecture her. However, the girl's mother has never actually stated any of this and the pair have never sat down and properly talked about it. Upon the girl finally revealing her ambition, the mother is delighted to hear she's found a career that makes her happy and never expected her to have any involvement in the family business.

How many times have you talked to a person and the conversation you ended up having was very different from what you thought it would be?

Stick to the facts, try not to read too deeply into another person's mind and only take in what another person says or does, not what you think that they think.

DON'T WORRY ABOUT WHAT OTHERS THINK

Part of putting yourself first is living your life the *way you want to live it and not how you think others want you to live it*. Students can feel lots of pressure during exam time because of their parents or friends, from expectations actually stated to assumed and imagined ones.

First, we all think about our own lives much more than anyone else's. We don't spend long intricately thinking about what other people think and do. If you worry about what someone else thinks of you, chances are they weren't thinking very much at all.

Next, does what someone else thinks of you change who you are? Does a thought change the world? It is very good to be polite and considerate to others, yes, but also stand up for your beliefs.

Do not worry about what others think about you. Live your life your way and not anybody else's. What makes *your world* better is most important.

TRUST YOURSELF

As children we can believe our parents and other adults or older people are always right. As we get older, it can be difficult to let go of this belief and accept that when it comes to our own lives, we know better.

What you believe is best for you, *is* best for you. Trust your own judgment. Trust your own decision making.

List times you did what somebody else said and regretted it, then list times you did something others said not to do that turned out great. If you remember decisions where you felt your decision was wrong, find the positives, such as the lesson you learned from that experience that you otherwise may not have learned.

WHAT WE FEEL AND WHAT WE ARE

Just because we *feel* something, doesn't mean we *are* something.

If you feel guilty, that doesn't mean you actually are guilty of something. If you feel useless, worthless or hopeless, that doesn't mean you are useless, worthless or hopeless.

Don't use your emotions as justification or proof, stick to the facts.

COMPARING YOURSELF TO OTHERS

As we have already established, nobody is exactly the same as you, so comparing yourself to others isn't always going to work.

Everybody has a different combination of what they do well and what they don't do so well. Everybody is given different opportunities. Everybody receives luck in different ways. Everybody is on their own unique journey that you can't compare with yours. Focus on *your* journey and how you feel it is going.

Sometimes comparing yourself to others does have its benefits. For example, it's good not to have a double standard; where the standard for yourself is very harsh compared the standard you expect from someone else.

Progress is important but often there are other and better ways to measure it than by comparing yourself to others.

IT'S NOT YOU, IT'S THEM. HONESTLY

When you have an argument with somebody, it is very easy to feel guilty or responsible. I found it tough to learn that it if I had difficulty with a person, it was not always my fault. It might not be my problem but theirs.

Yes, look inwards to identify what you may have done and how much you may be responsible, especially if you are having the same problems with many different people.

However, *also* look outwards and identify how others (or the universe) may be at fault too, especially if it is only them you are consistently having an issue with.

Remember that other people can have black and white thoughts, may focus on the negative, try to read minds and so on just like you may do too.

If you argue with your partner about keeping the house clean, it's possible that you are very untidy. On the other hand, your partner may be rather obsessive about cleaning.

If you are having difficulty with a person, it is one of the more acceptable times to compare yourself with others. You may look at yourself and think, "My cleaning standards are quite similar to my friends' and peers' ones" then look at your partner and think, "Yet my partner compared to them is really compulsive" and realise that your partner's cleaning standards are overly high instead of yours being exceedingly low.

UNKINDNESS STARTS WITH INSECURITY

When someone is unkind to you or bullies you, you can think, "I must have done something wrong" or "Is there something wrong with me?"

One of the most difficult lessons for me to take to heart, in part because it sounds so cliché, was that such people are mean and hurtful because they are insecure.

Bullies and cruel people have issues and to some extent feel worthless in some way. When they are nasty to you, it is because they think you have something that they want: happiness, intelligence, talent, (a kind) family, motivation, friends, freedom, attractiveness, success, health, wealth, luck, a future and much, much more.

They feel intimidated by you, they feel jealous of you, they may even think of you as a threat. Rather than trying to go up to your level, they try bringing you down to theirs. Instead of going for what is right, they go for what is easy.

Make a list of times people were not nice to you and find the ways they may have only had a little in life where you had a lot (feel free to use the list I provided before). You may only identify one quality or attribute that you had and that they didn't, it may even seem small to you, yet that one thing is the world to them and is what they were scared of most of all.

It's not personal. It's not about you. It's about them.

GIVING THE BENEFIT OF THE DOUBT

When you meet someone, you may not like or get along with them at first. They may initially put you off after being a bit rude or inconsiderate.

At the time, that person may have been dealing with something important or difficult. Given they don't even know you, it is unlikely they are being personal. You never know what is going through somebody's head or going on in their life.

Similarly, if you meet a person who comes across as a bit cold and distant, remember that they could be shy. It may not be that a person dislikes you, but rather that they may struggle to warm up to other people.

As you meet people, try to bear in mind that some will be less comfortable being around people than others. Some people will be more in-tune with other peoples' emotions than others.

Give the benefit of the doubt and give people a second chance. It's only when people are consistently unkind that you might want to make efforts to remove them from your life.

First impressions aren't always perfect. It can take time to find out who a person really is and whether they are someone you want in your life. There are many ways friendships and relationships can begin. Strong friendships can often have unexpected starts.

STICK TO THE RIGHT PEOPLE

Some people will understand certain parts of your life better than others, such as your career, relationships, family, health, wealth and so on.

A friend without kids may not understand the problems you are facing with yours. Someone from the corporate world who doesn't get show business may not be able to help their actor friend. Try to figure out who understands you in what ways so you know who is best to support you in certain situations. When you have a problem, try to only talk to people who "get it".

Overall, the people you love, who bring out the best in you and make you feel better about life are brilliant people that you want to keep in your life and stick to.

There are people however, who are not good for you. These people make you anxious, depressed, angry, bring out the worst in you, stress you out, are demanding and bring you down. These are not people you want to keep in your life. Helping them isn't your pleasure, it's a chore.

If you lived without someone before, you can live without them again. Don't be afraid to cut out those who make your life worse, even if they are your "friends" or family.

DEALING WITH DIFFICULT PEOPLE

There are some people you just can't remove from your life. Sometimes, you have to deal with a difficult person.

Such people can be very argumentative and opinionated. An effective way of coping with them is to find some detail in what they say that you can agree with. Things can get tense if you suddenly react defensively. By finding a way to agree with them, you can then start to make a case for your opinion and because you didn't outright say that they were wrong, they may be more open to listening.

Some people however, can be incredibly stubborn. Don't get into a debate with such people, as you can't win. Find the agreeable bits and try to just move on. Lots of people simply like provoking reactions, which gets them attention, so when they realise they are not provoking a big reaction out of you, they may even stop.

TAKING CRITICISM

When you receive criticism, it can be hard not to take it personally and feel bad about it. Here are some important questions to consider when receiving criticism:

Is this person important to me?

Is what they are saying rational?

Did they give *constructive* criticism?

Is there an insecurity they might have?

How much am I responsible?

For a start, do you like the person or even know them? Is their opinion one that you value? If not, you can just brush it off. Otherwise, think about what they said.

Is what they said rational? Was it a fair comment or did they use black and white language, predict the future, exaggerate, read someone's mind and so on? You can't take them as seriously if their statement was flawed.

Did you feel they were trying to help? Did they give some constructive criticism, state it gently or give you some compliments as well? Or were they just kind of ruthless? If they went about it in a good way, remember that they are just trying to help and are doing it because they care. If they were just nasty, remember the next question…

Could they be insecure at all? Could making you feel worse benefit them in some way? Depending on what your relationship to them is and what the criticism was about, they may feel jealous or threatened by you and be trying to bring you down.

Finally, find a way to agree. List the ways you are responsible, how something could be your fault or how what they are saying is true. Then also list how it's not your fault and how they are wrong.

Oh, and don't forget that they might just be going through a difficult time or be mad at something else instead. It really may not be personal at all. It usually isn't.

OTHER PEOPLE ASKING FOR ADVICE

When other people ask for our advice and then do something different from what we told them, we can get frustrated and take it personally.

For a start, other peoples' decisions and actions are out of our control, so it's not worth getting worked up about them.

Next, they are not actually asking you to make their decision for them. All they want is outside perspective. They want your advice and input to help them make the decision themselves. Be pleased that they valued your opinion since they asked you for it.

Finally, when we have decisions to make, there can be an option that deep down inside we are secretly leaning towards. When we ask other people, we are looking for those answers that support the decision we want to make and don't want to hear the ones that go against that.

RESPECTING OTHER PEOPLES' WISHES

When you offer something to someone, don't get pushy or stubborn. If you ask someone if they want something and they refuse, don't keep asking them. It is okay to throw in a, "Are you sure?" or "I really don't mind doing it" afterwards but if they refuse a second time, drop it. Don't make someone feel like their decision is wrong.

If you are in someone else's home or business and they set some rules or if someone is doing you a favour and they make a few small requests: follow them – even if they are not what you normally would do. If someone says don't clean anything up in their house: *don't*. They may have a system or a particular way of doing things. If someone is paying for a meal and they tell you to start eating when your food arrives first, do it. Again, you can ask, "Are you sure?" or "Is that okay?" but don't push it. You may be trying to not be rude but by ignoring their request, you are (ironically) being rude.

SHOULD, MUST, NEED TO AND OUGHT TO

Language is very powerful. Changing just one word in a sentence can change the impact of it immensely. If you say that you *should* do something, it implies you *have to* do it and it creates an obligation. If you then don't do this now *required* task, you feel guilty and disappointed in yourself.

People say things like, "Oh, I should have called my mum yesterday" or "I must study" or "I need to go to the gym today" or "I ought to look for a new job". Ponder this: do you *absolutely have to* do any of these things? Does it need to be done *today*? Is there a law that says you *must*? Will the world explode if you don't?

Remember this: you *don't absolutely have to do these things* but they can be nice things to do. In fact, it's good that you are even thinking of doing these things. Lots of people don't care much about their mothers, exams, health or career. You don't *have to* call your mum, but it just might brighten her day (and maybe yours too) if you did. You don't have to study, but it does help in general and winging exams isn't really a good idea.

A lot of the pressure we feel is actually pressure we put on ourselves. We tend to mind-read expectations of us or follow loose, unwritten rules in society that lead to "should-thinking".

Even saying please and thank you is not any kind of requirement. I'm *not* saying to stop saying please and thank you. What I am saying is don't be hard on yourself if you forget to.

If something is about life and death, you should do it. If something is the law you should do it. If something is a rule in a competition or place, you should do it. Otherwise, really question whether something is necessary or not. Ask *why*?

Try to eliminate these bad words, they can be very dangerous. If you *actually have to do* something, say that you *have to* and if you don't, instead use phrases such as:

It might be nice to…

It would be good if…

It may be preferable to…

It could be better if…

It won't do me any harm to...

PERFECTION

If there isn't much in the world that is totally one way or totally the other, then for the most part, perfection doesn't really exist.

There is always more you can do, always an improvement that can be made. A room cannot be perfectly clean, a race can be run a bit faster and food can taste a little nicer. Don't forever chase something that you cannot catch.

Conversely, this means there is no such thing as a total disaster, things can also always be a little bit worse. A dirtier room, a slower run race and food that may not taste nice but at least isn't burnt. So don't beat yourself up about anything you don't consider a success.

Surely getting ten out of ten on a test is perfect? Yes... and no. You may get a perfect ten but how quickly did you complete the test? Was there a question you got a bit stuck on? Did you cross out and replace any answers? Could your answers or even your handwriting have been a little bit clearer?

Once again, on the flip side, if you got zero out of ten on a test, you may find that some of your answers were quite close. If you put "King Henry VII" instead of "King Henry VIII" that's a much better answer than "Cheese".

Some things do need to be closer to perfect than others: such as surgery, but most others don't. Sit down and try to think of all the ways the world is not perfect so that you can let go of any need to do things perfectly.

SUCCESS, PERFECTION AND FUN

We like to achieve and enjoy succeeding. Often the better we do at something, the better we feel afterwards. So it's understandable if you feel you can't enjoy something unless you win or do well or even unless things end perfectly. However, this simply isn't true.

Think back and list all the times you haven't succeeded or weren't perfect, yet you still enjoyed yourself. In the past you may have lost whilst playing a sport or game yet still had lots of fun. Conversely, think of things that you enjoy doing, then think of how you don't always do them perfectly. You may enjoy baking despite the fact that your cakes aren't always immaculate.

Have you ever strived for perfection and slightly obsessed over something? Times where you had something ninety-nine percent right but then spent far too long getting that final one percent? Were those times fun?

Your happiness is not reliant on your success.

SUCCESS VS TIME AND EFFORT

For some tasks, achieving the first ninety percent is a lot simpler and less time-consuming than completing the remaining ten percent.

Imagine cleaning a room. If you simply vacuum the floors and wipe the surfaces, the room is largely clean and this does not take too long. It's only cleaning the few areas that remain afterwards that make the task much more lengthy and difficult. To get the room cleaner, you need to start moving furniture, emptying cabinets, getting on your knees or climbing up on stools, sorting your possessions and getting extra equipment.

Now imagine that you have to clean six rooms. What sounds more successful: cleaning six rooms ninety percent well or one room ninety-nine percent well? It kind of equates to five hundred and forty percent success versus ninety nine percent success. In the time it takes to clean a room with ninety-nine percent success, how many could you clean with ninety percent success?

MISTAKES ARE UNAVOIDABLE AND NECESSARY

Fear of making a mistake can be holding you back from what you want to do. It's understandable that we want to do something well right from the start. However, this is not realistic.

We don't know everything when we start out, so we can't really expect to be perfect. Is anybody born brilliant at something? Sportspeople? Performers? No. Everything that's worth doing in life takes at least *some* work. Have the same brilliant people *never* made *any* mistakes at all? No.

If perfection doesn't really exist, then mistakes, errors and imperfections are always going to happen in some form to everybody. Once you truly accept this, you can relax.

Also remember that mistakes teach us lessons. Often the best and most effective lessons we learn stem from those mistakes and bad experiences.

WHAT SUCCESS MEANS TO YOU

Success isn't being perfect or not making mistakes. Once you accept this, suddenly you have a much wider definition of what success is, as more outcomes can be classed as successful ones. Before, only ten out of ten may have been deemed a success, but now nine, eight, seven and six may be included. Even a five or lower could be deemed very successful, if seeing what you got wrong helps you next time to get things right.

In addition to this, not everything is either a straight-up success or a total failure; there is middle-ground and there are lots of different types of success that you will want to recognise.

Letting go of perfectionism also makes it easier to figure out what success means to you whenever you take on a task.

For example, what does it mean to be a successful actor? Is it winning an Oscar? Appearing on Broadway? Working with a particular director? Making all of your income by acting? Or simply being happy?

Different people have different ideas of what success is, and that's awesome. In order to chase after your dreams, you want to figure out what success means to you.

GOALS AND DREAMS

With goals and dreams, you still want to try to be specific and make things measurable wherever possible. Similarly, breaking down everything into steps, stages and types helps immensely too. A goal needs to be realistic; otherwise it will not be achievable.

Don't turn your goal or any parts of it into a "should" unless it is necessary – such as if a certain career path requires a degree or qualification. In particular, don't let your goal be because it's what someone else wants. Don't let anybody else dictate your dreams and don't live your life based on an expectation of you or because of a "potential" you have.

Always keep the focus on fun and always try to make everything as enjoyable as possible, focus on the positives.

Your goals may change as you move along the path, life can throw some pretty interesting things at you and dreams can transform. So don't forget to review your goals and change them when necessary.

QUITTING IS OKAY

Provided you have given something a good try, there is absolutely nothing wrong with quitting.

Don't quit just because something is difficult. If you truly want something that is realistic and brings happiness to your life, go for it and don't give in.

But if you realise you don't want to do something anymore, if it is consistently making you miserable, stressing you out and impeding your life, stop doing it.

If you try something and discover it doesn't make you happy or that it is not what you thought it was, there is no shame in quitting. If you try something long enough to reasonably evaluate that the effort far outweighs the reward and that it is just not worth it, don't do it.

Don't worry about what other people may think. You know yourself better than anyone.

TIME LIMITS

Lots of people will say to set an effective goal, set a time limit or deadline. However, I advise you to generally avoid doing this if you can.

If a person wanted to lose ten pounds in a month and at the end of it they lost nine pounds that is an amazing accomplishment. Yet there could be a part of them that feels quite disappointed. Some may even feel the whole thing was a failure because they didn't reach their target. Without the time constraint they would feel more joy and think, "Just one more pound!" Also, those times when we all inevitably slip back a little aren't so bad when a clock isn't ticking away.

The other reason I advise against time constraints is when we set a goal, it is usually to do something that we have never done before. If we have never really done something before, we are not very good at estimating how long it takes to do it. It takes time to figure out how something works and what it is really like.

Even with a recommended guideline, lots of things take a bit longer when we start out, such as the time to cook a recipe.

If you want to enter a particular marathon or fit into a dress before a wedding, then that's fine and time can be a good motivator. But if your goal is a bit more general, don't worry about time.

If after a while you find you are not very reliable when it comes to accomplishing your goal, then you can set some deadlines as a motivator, as by then you will have a better idea of what a realistic deadline is.

SET THE BAR LOW AND AIM HIGH

Make your goals basic; don't make perfection the only acceptable outcome. There is a difference between what you want and what you want the most.

In exams, I always focused on what I needed to pass, instead of what I needed for the top grade. Thinking I needed to know only forty percent of a subject instead of seventy or eighty percent helped relieve an immense amount of pressure.

Setting the bar low allows you to be happier with more outcomes. Plus it allows you to more easily look at what you have done rather than what you have yet to do. It is better to see how much better you are doing (than a pass) rather than how far off you are (from an A).

Similarly, if you set your target to be less than what you achieved last time, you know it is something you can realistically achieve. That sense of completing your goal gives you the energy and motivation to push further.

I am *not* saying only do the minimal amount of work nor am I saying to have low expectations. Always try hard, try to beat your records and always try to do your best. This is just to help you have a positive mindset, cope better with any potential disappointment and lessen the burden. It's better to have these types of "prepare for the worst and hope for the best" or "anything else is icing on the cake" approaches.

THE POSITIVES OF YOUR GOAL

An immediate motivator to achieve a task or goal is to write out all the different ways your life will improve by achieving your goal or completing that task.

Visualise all of the positive ways your life will change once you achieve your goal. It is much better to focus on the positives of achieving your goal than the negatives of not achieving it.

If your goal is to lose weight, think of how being slimmer will help you live longer, how you will be able to do more physically, how you will feel healthier, how you may become more attractive to others, the renewed confidence you will have and the improved self-image you will have as well.

IF IT TAKES TWO MINUTES – DO IT NOW

Often, there are lots of little things we would like to do. If you think something you want to do will take less than two minutes, do it straight away.

It's the little things that make up life and doing lots of these little jobs will give you a strong sense of accomplishment. These small tasks also occupy a lot of headspace and nag at us when they remain undone.

If you can't do a two minute task right now, do it as soon as you get the chance to. If two minutes is too long, shorten it to one minute. If you can do five minutes, extend it to that. Essentially, follow the principle that if something is quick to do, then do it right away.

MOTIVATION FOLLOWS ACTION

We tend to believe we need to have loads of motivation first before we can do anything. However, it's the opposite that is actually more accurate.

Though it's true we need a little bit of motivation to start something, it's after we start doing something that we have some success, realise it is not so hard or feel that it is actually kind of fun, which energises us.

Knowing your next step provides great relief; doing it provides you with motivation and often even enough to keep you going until the end.

PROCRASTINATION AND GETTING GOING

It can be really tough sometimes to get started on something and on some days you just really won't be feeling it.

For a start, don't overwhelm yourself by looking at everything you haven't done or by giving yourself too much to do. Don't feel that you *have to* do everything right away.

After that, break your task into as many small steps as possible. Try to make each step as quick and easy to do as possible, particularly the first one. If any steps can be completed with the two minute rule, that's great.

If you're cleaning your house for example, don't just break it up into upstairs and downstairs or even by rooms. Break each room into simple areas.

After doing two minutes you will probably find that they went by very quickly and feel like continuing.

LOCK YOURSELF INTO ACTION

When a task or goal requires a lot of work – even after breaking it all down – the fear of doing it all can take hold. When this happens, you want to try and find an action in which once you take it, the rest will naturally follow.

When I first went to America, it was for a convention. I really wanted to go and knew that it was a great next step in my career. Yet, I was overwhelmed by how many decisions there were to make: accommodation, flights (I had never been on a plane before), visas, a passport, the trip's length and so much more. It was so daunting that it almost put me off going entirely.

However, I realised if I registered for the convention, I was locked in. Soon I would have to make some decisions about how long the trip would be, which would help me book flights and the hotel, once I had a flight I would need the passport and so on. It was an act that almost forced me to make some other decisions. Find these actions yourself, take them and just know that everything else will follow, everything will be all right.

DON'T WAIT FOR PERFECTION

Often we say, "I won't do that until…" and we want things to be just right when we first start something. Yes, occasionally there may be some times better than others to do things but there is never a perfect time to do anything.

For a start, the universe won't make everything just happen for us; there are things we have to do for ourselves. There are other things that we can't learn or prepare for until we are actually doing it. Don't worry about things not being great right away. Nobody expects perfection from someone starting out. Take very little steps but always move forward. Progress will just kind of happen if you take action.

Taking a jump into the unknown can be scary. However, we learn from new experiences and the mistakes we make. Sometimes in order to achieve our goals, we have to do things we are less comfortable with.

DON'T BE AFRAID TO ASK OTHERS FOR HELP

We can feel uncomfortable asking others for help. We may: feel we are being a burden or wasting other peoples' time; fear they may think we are stupid for asking; feel like we don't need help and can do it by ourselves or we may feel that it doesn't count if other people help us.

Everyone who has achieved their dreams has received some help along the way. Those who are successful once needed help themselves and they understand that. They still had to do most of the leg work for themselves, just as you will have to as well.

People like helping other people; it gives them a sense of self-satisfaction. A person won't help you if they don't want to or if they don't have the time to do so. If they are helping you it means you are not being a burden. You never know if you don't ask.

Once a person says yes to you, don't over-explain, apologise or keep asking. You've already made your sale, so just thank them.

FEARLESSNESS AND COURAGE

Fear is the number one reason for inaction. It can stand in the way of beneficial changes. We can fear doing things that we don't want to do, as well as things that we do want to do.

It is not that you must be fearless to take action, but rather, you want to be courageous. Fearlessness means to have no fear at all. Courage is feeling fear but carrying on anyway.

Courage to some may be a word reserved for firemen and soldiers but don't feel that your problems are inadequate. Everyone has their own personal battles and relatively speaking, your issues are just as important as anyone else's.

The devotion a task may require and how much effort we may need to put in can be scary. Remember that it takes a lot of effort to make something look effortless and that only you can change your world.

TEST WHAT YOU "CAN'T DO"

If you think to yourself, "I can't do that" then set up an experiment. Take what you believe you can't do, break it into those all-important, small, gradual steps and try doing them as a test.

You'll be surprised at what you actually can do. Maybe you won't accomplish all the steps, but you may have done more of them than what you thought.

If you are a student and say, "I can't revise" then just sit down and read some notes for thirty seconds. That's all. Feel that was easy? Read for a minute, then two, then five. Test your limits.

CHALLENGE YOUR PREDICTIONS AND BELIEFS

In addition to thinking you cannot do something, there are lots of other predictions that you may make. You may think a task will be difficult or won't be enjoyable or that you won't be successful.

Pick such an activity and break it down into smaller steps. Predict what you think the difficulty of each step will be as a percentage *before* doing it, then do the activity and *afterwards* write down what you felt the actual difficulty was, also as a percentage.

Hopefully you'll often find the actual difficulty (AD) to be lower than your predicted difficulty (PD). You can also test predicted enjoyment (PE) versus actual enjoyment (AE) and predicted success (PS) versus actual success (AS) in a similar way.

Maybe you think that because something is difficult means it won't be fun or that something cannot be fun if you are not successful.

Similarly, if you think a task will take a long time, estimate how long you think it takes and then see how long it actually takes. For anything measurable, guess what you think will happen and then measure what actually happens, such as the number of times you will successfully do something.

If you keep putting off cleaning your house, your table might look something like this:

Activity	**PD**	**AD**
Clean Lounge	98%	40%
1. Tidy coffee table in lounge	20%	5%
2. Dust lounge surfaces	30%	10%
3. Vacuum lounge rug	50%	15%
4. Vacuum the rest of the lounge floor	70%	55%
...	...	...

Or if you want to see if you can still enjoy yourself regardless of how many miles you can run before you have to stop, you may have a table like this:

Activity	PE	AE	PS	AS
Jogging	5%	60%	0.2	0.5

Any negative consequence that you may predict from taking action can be tested in this way – not just in terms of enjoyment, difficulty or success. Do a trial, stick it out until the very end and see what happens.

USE A COUNTER

A good way to cut down negative thoughts is to use an old-fashioned counter; they can be bought cheaply on the internet and there are apps for phones and tablets. Every time you catch yourself having a negative thought, click the counter. At the end of each day, make a note of your total.

At first, as you become more aware of your negative thoughts and notice them more often, you might find that the number goes up. But soon afterwards, as you continue to catch yourself and correct those thoughts, it will go down.

The counter can be used for a specific kind of negative thought instead of general ones. You could press the button each time you say the word "should" or a pre-emptive sorry, each time you try to read someone's mind or use black/white language and so on.

Any bad habit that you want to reduce can be greatly helped by using the counter. Conversely, you could use it in an effort to increase the frequency of any good habit too, such as each time you look for a win-win.

ARGUE WITH YOURSELF

We have talked a lot about the irrational thinking that brings you down and the beliefs you have that hold you back. They may be automatic thoughts that come thick and fast.

Tackle these thoughts and find the truth using a table to argue back rationally at each irrational thought. Think of what advice you would give to a friend if these were their thoughts.

Here is an example of a student who doesn't want to revise:

Thought	Challenge
I don't feel like it.	You are very, very unlikely to ever actually want to revise in the first place.
It reminds me of exams.	True, but you are probably going to keep thinking about exams and how you're not working for them if you don't do something.
I will realise how little I know.	Everyone has to start somewhere, the only way you are going to learn and memorise the material is by putting in the work.
I can start tomorrow.	This argument could be used until the day before your exam. You don't have to do much; even doing a little will help and give you a great sense of accomplishment.
I can't stand loads.	Then just do 5 minutes of revision and build it up gradually.

PROS AND CONS

Writing a classic pros and cons list can be incredibly useful. They are helpful in two different scenarios:

When you are feeling completely unsure of what to do.

When you kind of already know what to do but want some extra help and to see it written out.

Ensure that you really exhaust all of your options when compiling these lists. Don't rush them. If you get stuck, walk away for a while. Somewhere in the back of your mind, you will come up with more ideas. Questions such as these are good to consider with a pros and cons list:

What will I do?

Would stopping/starting something help me?

Is it useful to think that?

Is it helpful to feel this way?

Is this belief realistic?

IMPROVED ACTION

Once you notice the negative thoughts, behaviours and beliefs discussed throughout this book you will naturally want to remove them or turn them into more positive ones.

I feel there are three steps to this:

Noticing

Caring/Apologising

Repeating

First, you actually have to notice a bad thing to be able to change it.

Second, be kind to yourself. Don't beat yourself up for making a mistake and if you do, apologise to yourself. Praise yourself for noticing the error.

Finally, don't just say, "I'll do it better next time" or partially do the action the preferred way. Instead, immediately go back to the beginning and repeat the action in its entirety in a more desirable way.

If you want to stop saying or thinking the word "should" then first you want to catch yourself saying or thinking it. Don't be cruel to yourself, just think, "Right, let's try that again" and then repeat the sentence you said but altering it so that you don't say the word "should" in it.

This can be used for any action, not just one related to happiness and positivity.

Let's pretend that you want to start closing the door after you go downstairs. If one day you notice a while later that you forgot, don't insult yourself or just close it. Instead, be nice to yourself, go back upstairs and then walk down and close the door. Repeat the *full* action, as this will help it become fixed into your memory.

CORE BELIEFS AND FUNDAMENTAL WANTS

Following the tips in this book and doing the exercises will help you deal with your problems and increase your happiness. But to increase the chances of your problems not only going away but staying away, you will want to deal with your core beliefs and fundamental wants.

A core belief is something deep inside that you accept as true about yourself, about others and/or the world. A fundamental want is something you want from yourself, others or the world in general. Sometimes one affects the other. These convictions are carried with you in everything you do. They influence your thinking and your actions. Some are good. Others are not so good.

A person who at their core believes they are worthless may say that they feel their job is not worthwhile. Using this book, they may realise that *their job* is worthwhile... but if they did not realise that *they themselves are worthwhile*, getting fired from that job could devastate them.

A person who fundamentally wants to not be a disappointment to others may frequently offer to help people and say yes to other peoples' demands, even if it's not at all convenient for them. They could develop an issue with perfectionism and a fear of failure. Identifying that want could lead to a realisation that they believe they are inferior to other people. A person who doesn't want to be arrogant may go so far the other way that they develop low self-esteem.

Your automatic thoughts can be a very good indicator of what your core beliefs and fundamental wants are. Any patterns, themes or consistencies you find in the exercises you do will also point you towards them. Some unhelpful core beliefs could be:

I am worthless	I am an idiot
Humanity is horrible	I don't deserve success
I can't achieve anything great	I can't have a good relationship
I should get As in all of my exams	I am not likable

Once you identify your beliefs and wants, try to pay attention to how your thoughts and actions are a reflection of them. You may find that doing the basic exercises, altering your language and shifting your mindset may be enough to change or remove a core belief or fundamental want. However, you may have to work long and hard on altering an undesired core belief to something more sensible.

As with all your thoughts, you want to question your core beliefs and fundamental wants:

Are they rational?

Are they helpful?

Do they make you happy?

You want to be realistic and avoid incorporating black/white language, mind reading, predicting the future, "should-thinking", exaggeration, labelling yourself entirely or falling into any of the other pitfalls discussed.

If your core belief or fundamental want doesn't actually help you – if it doesn't motivate you, calm you down, give you hope or anything else that leads to happiness – then you will want to change it.

Finding out who you truly are and what you really believe can be one of the scariest things you ever do... but is also one of the very best.

CONCLUSION

Parts of this will sound simple and make sense to you. Parts of it will sound difficult and be confusing. Happiness and maintaining it comes to some people easier than it does to others. Everyone has different genes and experiences. When it comes to your happiness, don't get preoccupied with the world or with other people; focus purely on yourself.

Your emotions stem from your thoughts. Even small changes in your language and the way you think about things can have a massively positive impact. Remember that though happiness is not a choice, it is a way of life and *that* is a choice.

It is my hope that there is something in this book that will help you. Don't just read it once; information at the end could help you better understand concepts from the beginning. It can help you in bad times and in good ones. I wish you all the very best on your personal journey to happiness.

THANKS

Firstly, thank you to everyone who has bought and read this book. I am incredibly grateful to you.

I wish to thank my family for being so loving and supportive, particularly: Rick, Jane, Todd and Lane, plus Anne and Jim.

Thank you to my best friends: William, James, Charlie, Lewis and especially Finn – who helped me tremendously with redrafting this book.

I am very grateful to Olympia Publishing for all the great work they've done publishing this book and to Ben and Tilly for putting me in contact with Olympia in the first place.

I am very thankful to Penny Abshire for both her wonderful foreword and for all of her amazing support.

I also want to say thank you to my mentors for teaching me so much, not just in my career but about life too. Thanks to Bill, Richard, Crispin and Rob for all that they've taught me.

Finally, thank you to anyone who has made me smile, laugh or made me feel good about myself. I wouldn't be where I am without you.